We hope this book has been informative and helpful on your journey to understanding and celebrating older adults. Thank you for your interest and support!

Title: The Roots of Net-Busting-Exploring the Early Days of Football's Best Goal Scorers

Subtitle: The Fierce and Historic Battles of Football's Rivalries

Series: Striking Gold: Top Scorers in Football before the 1980s

By Michael Jaynes

"Football is a simple game. Twenty-two men chase a ball for 90 minutes and at the end, the Germans always win."
Gary Lineker

"Some people think football is a matter of life and death. I assure you, it's much more serious than that."
Bill Shankly

"Football was different back then. It was more about the love of the game and the joy of scoring goals than it was about money and fame."
Pele

"The early days of football were a magical time. There was a purity to the sport that has been lost in modern times."
Bobby Charlton

"The great goal scorers of the past were true artists. They had a sense of poetry and beauty that is rarely seen in the game today."
Eusebio

"The goal scorers of the past were not just great athletes, they were also great storytellers. They could create drama and tension with every shot they took."
Nándor Hidegkuti

"The ball is round, the game lasts 90 minutes, and everything else is just theory."
Josef Herberger

Table of Contents

Introduction
Overview of the book's theme

Football is a sport that has captivated the hearts of millions across the globe for over a century. One of the most exciting aspects of the game is the art of goal scoring. The ability to score goals is what separates the great players from the good ones, and it is what has made legends out of some of the game's biggest stars.

In this book, we delve into the early years of some of the greatest goal scorers in football history. From the humble beginnings of their careers to their rise to fame, readers will gain a deeper understanding of what it takes to become a prolific goal scorer. With detailed accounts of each player's career highlights, personal struggles, and notable achievements, this book offers a comprehensive look at the roots of their success.

The book is divided into six chapters, each focusing on a different player. We begin with Ferenc Puskas, the Hungarian legend who is widely regarded as one of the greatest players of all time. Puskas' success with Budapest Honved and Real Madrid is legendary, and his international career was nothing short of remarkable.

We then move on to Ademir de Menezes, the Brazilian goal-scoring machine who led his country to World Cup glory in 1950. Ademir's rise to fame with Vasco da Gama and his success with the Brazilian national team make him one of the most fascinating players in the history of the game.

Gunnar Nordahl, the Swedish striker who was a goal-scoring machine for AC Milan, is the subject of our third chapter. Nordahl's success in Italy and his international career with Sweden make him a player who is revered to this day.

The fourth chapter focuses on István Nyers, another Hungarian who was a goal-scoring machine for MTK Budapest in the 1940s and 50s. Nyers' remarkable record for both club and country makes him a player who is worthy of recognition.

Denis Law, the Scottish striker who was a goal-scoring sensation for Huddersfield Town, Manchester City, and Manchester United, is the subject of our fifth chapter. Law's international career with Scotland and his later years with Manchester City make him a player who is remembered fondly by fans around the world.

Finally, we turn our attention to Nat Lofthouse, the legendary Bolton Wanderers striker who was known for his incredible physicality and his ability to find the back of the net. Lofthouse's international career with England and his later years with Bolton Wanderers make him a player who is revered by fans to this day.

By exploring the early years of these six players, we hope to provide readers with a deeper understanding of what it takes to become a prolific goal scorer. Whether you are a die-hard fan of the game or simply enjoy reading about inspiring journeys, the "Roots of" series is sure to captivate and inspire.

Football is undoubtedly one of the most popular sports in the world, with millions of fans following their favorite teams and players on a daily basis. However, while fans often focus on current players and events, it's important not to forget the rich history of the sport. The early years of football have shaped the game as we know it today, and studying football history can provide valuable insights into how the sport has evolved over time.

One of the primary reasons why studying football history is important is that it helps us understand how the game has changed over time. The sport of football has undergone significant changes since its early days, including changes to the rules, the format of competitions, and the playing styles of teams and players. By studying the history of football, we can gain a deeper understanding of how and why these changes occurred, and how they have impacted the sport as a whole.

In addition to understanding the evolution of the game, studying football history also allows us to appreciate the achievements of past players and teams. Football has produced countless legends over the years, many of whom are still remembered and revered today. By learning about the careers of these players and the teams they played for, we can gain a greater appreciation for their accomplishments and understand why they are so highly regarded.

Another important aspect of studying football history is that it can help us contextualize current events in the sport. By understanding the history of football, we can better appreciate the significance of current players and events, and understand how they fit into the broader narrative of the sport. This can be particularly valuable for fans who are new to the sport, as it can help them get up to speed on the history and context of the game.

Finally, studying football history can be a source of inspiration for players and fans alike. Many of the greatest players in the history of the sport have had to overcome significant challenges and obstacles to achieve success, and their stories can be a source of motivation and inspiration for those looking to follow in their footsteps. By learning about the struggles and triumphs of past players, we can gain a greater appreciation for the dedication and perseverance required to succeed in football.

In conclusion, studying football history is an important undertaking for anyone who wants to gain a deeper understanding of the sport. By learning about the evolution of the game, the achievements of past players and teams, and the context of current events, we can become better fans and gain a greater appreciation for the sport as a whole.

In this book, we will be exploring the early years of some of the greatest goal scorers in football history. Each player featured in this book has left an indelible mark on the game, and their contributions to football are still celebrated to this day. In this section, we will provide a brief explanation of the players featured in this book and highlight some of their notable achievements.

The first player we will be exploring is Ferenc Puskas. Puskas was a Hungarian forward who scored an incredible 706 goals during his career, making him one of the all-time greats. He rose to fame playing for Budapest Honved and later Real Madrid, where he helped the team win multiple European Cups. Puskas was known for his incredible left foot and his ability to score from almost any position on the field.

Next, we will be exploring the career of Ademir de Menezes, a Brazilian forward who scored 413 goals during his career. Ademir rose to fame playing for Vasco da Gama, where he helped the team win multiple state championships. He also played for the Brazilian national team, where he helped the team win the 1950 World Cup.

We will also be exploring the career of Gunnar Nordahl, a Swedish forward who scored 369 goals during his career. Nordahl is best known for his time playing for AC

Milan, where he helped the team win multiple Serie A titles. He was also a prolific scorer for the Swedish national team, helping the team reach the final of the 1958 World Cup.

István Nyers is another Hungarian forward we will be exploring in this book. Nyers scored 351 goals during his career, most notably for MTK Budapest. He was known for his incredible ball control and his ability to score from almost any position on the field.

Denis Law is a Scottish forward who scored 350 goals during his career. He rose to fame playing for Manchester United, where he helped the team win multiple domestic and European titles. Law also played for the Scottish national team, where he was known for his incredible skill and agility on the field.

Finally, we will be exploring the career of Nat Lofthouse, an English forward who scored 285 goals during his career. Lofthouse is best known for his time playing for Bolton Wanderers, where he helped the team win the FA Cup in 1958. He also played for the English national team, where he was known for his incredible strength and heading ability.

Each of these players had a unique journey to becoming one of football's greatest goal scorers. In this book, we will explore their early years and the factors that contributed to their success. By understanding the roots of

their success, we can gain a deeper appreciation for the game
and the players who have shaped it over the years.

Early life and career beginnings

Ferenc Puskás, widely regarded as one of the greatest football players of all time, was born on April 2, 1927, in Budapest, Hungary. From an early age, Puskás showed an aptitude for football, often playing in the streets with his friends. He was a gifted athlete and soon caught the attention of his local football club, Kispest AC.

Puskás joined Kispest AC's youth team at the age of 12, where he began to hone his skills as a striker. He quickly rose through the ranks and made his debut for the senior team at the age of 16 in 1943. Puskás proved to be a natural goalscorer, scoring 9 goals in 5 games in his debut season.

At the age of 18, Puskás was called up to the Hungarian national team, making his debut in August 1945 against Austria. Over the next few years, he established himself as a key member of the national team, helping Hungary win the Central European International Cup in 1948 and 1953.

Puskás' success on the international stage attracted the attention of clubs from around Europe, including Real Madrid, who were looking to strengthen their squad ahead of the 1958 season. Despite initial resistance from Kispest AC,

Puskás eventually secured a transfer to the Spanish giants in 1958 for a then-world-record fee of £153,000.

Puskás' time at Real Madrid was marked by incredible success, as he formed part of one of the greatest teams in football history, known as the "Madrid Galacticos." Alongside other legendary players such as Alfredo Di Stefano and Francisco Gento, Puskás won numerous domestic and international titles, including five consecutive European Cups from 1956 to 1960.

Despite suffering from a number of injuries in his later years, Puskás continued to score goals at an impressive rate. He retired from football in 1966, having scored a total of 706 goals in his career, including 621 for his clubs and 85 for the Hungarian national team.

Throughout his career, Puskás was renowned for his exceptional skill on the ball, his deadly finishing ability, and his leadership on and off the pitch. He was a true legend of the game and remains an inspiration to aspiring footballers around the world.

Ferenc Puskas' time at Budapest Honved was one of the most remarkable periods in his career. Puskas began his career with Kispest AC, which later became known as Budapest Honved, at the age of 15. He quickly became a regular in the team and was an integral part of the club's rise to prominence.

In the 1949-1950 season, Budapest Honved won the Hungarian league title for the first time in their history, with Puskas contributing 50 goals to the campaign. The following season, the club retained the title, with Puskas scoring an incredible 33 goals in just 19 league matches.

Puskas was known for his incredible technique and dribbling ability, as well as his accurate and powerful shooting. His goalscoring record at Budapest Honved was nothing short of phenomenal, with 352 goals in just 341 matches for the club.

One of the most memorable moments of Puskas' time at Budapest Honved came in 1954 when the club won the European Cup. Puskas scored twice in the final against Stade de Reims, including a spectacular equalizer in the second half, as Budapest Honved won 3-2.

Puskas' success at Budapest Honved helped to establish him as one of the best players in the world at the time. He was a key figure in a team that dominated Hungarian football and achieved success on the European stage. His performances at the club also played a significant role in his selection for the Hungarian national team, where he would go on to achieve even greater success.

In many ways, Puskas' success with Budapest Honved set the tone for the rest of his career. His goalscoring exploits at the club demonstrated his incredible talent and provided a platform for him to achieve even greater things in the years that followed. Without his success at Budapest Honved, it is unlikely that Puskas would have gone on to become the global superstar that he is remembered as today.

Ferenc Puskas is widely considered one of the greatest footballers of all time, and his international career played a significant role in cementing this reputation. Puskas represented Hungary in 84 matches, scoring 84 goals in the process. He was an integral member of the legendary Hungarian team of the 1950s, known as the Mighty Magyars.

Puskas made his international debut for Hungary in 1945, at the age of just 18. He scored a goal in his very first game, a 5-2 victory over Austria. However, it wasn't until the early 1950s that Puskas truly made his mark on the international stage. Along with players such as Nandor Hidegkuti and Sandor Kocsis, Puskas helped to form one of the greatest attacking partnerships in football history.

In 1952, Hungary embarked on a tour of England, widely regarded as the home of football. The team's performances on this tour, particularly their 6-3 victory over England at Wembley Stadium, stunned the football world. Puskas was the star of the show, scoring two goals and showcasing his extraordinary skill and technique.

Over the next few years, Puskas and the Hungarian team went from strength to strength. They won Olympic gold in 1952, and in 1953 they defeated England again, this time by a scoreline of 6-1. This victory, known as the Match of the

Century, is widely regarded as one of the greatest performances in football history. Puskas scored twice and was once again the standout player on the pitch.

In the 1954 World Cup, Hungary were one of the favorites to win the tournament. Puskas was in outstanding form, scoring four goals in the group stage. However, in the final against West Germany, Puskas was carrying an injury and was not at his best. Despite this, he managed to score a goal, although it was controversially ruled out for offside.

Although Hungary ultimately lost the final, Puskas' performances throughout the tournament had been nothing short of extraordinary. He had cemented his place as one of the greatest players in the world, and his international career would continue to be a source of inspiration for generations to come.

Ferenc Puskas is best known for his success with Real Madrid, where he became a legend and helped to establish the club as one of the greatest in football history. Puskas joined Real Madrid in 1958, after Hungary's failed revolution against the Soviet Union.

Puskas' arrival at Real Madrid was highly anticipated, and he quickly proved himself as a valuable asset to the team. In his first season, he scored 20 goals in 24 matches, helping the team win the Spanish league title. He also led Real Madrid to their first European Cup victory in 1958, scoring four goals in the final against AC Milan.

Puskas continued to excel in the following seasons, forming a lethal partnership with fellow striker Alfredo Di Stefano. Together, they led Real Madrid to five consecutive European Cup titles from 1958 to 1962, a record that still stands to this day. During this period, Puskas scored an incredible 35 goals in 39 European Cup matches, cementing his status as one of the greatest players of all time.

Puskas was known for his powerful left foot, which he used to devastating effect. He had an incredible ability to find the back of the net from almost any position on the pitch, and he was equally adept at scoring with both power and finesse. Puskas' skills and achievements on the pitch earned him the nickname "The Galloping Major," a reference to his military service in Hungary.

Off the pitch, Puskas was known for his larger-than-life personality and his love of good food and wine. He was a popular figure among his teammates and fans alike, and his contributions to Real Madrid's success will always be remembered.

In 1966, at the age of 39, Puskas retired from professional football. His legacy, however, lives on. He is widely regarded as one of the greatest players in football history, and his impact on the sport cannot be overstated. Puskas' move to Real Madrid marked a turning point in the club's history, and his success paved the way for future generations of players to follow in his footsteps.

Introduction to Ademir de Menezes

Ademir de Menezes, also known as Ademir da Guia, was a Brazilian footballer who played as an attacking midfielder or forward. He was born on April 8, 1922, in Rio de Janeiro, Brazil, and started his football career with the club, Bangu. However, it was with Vasco da Gama, where Ademir achieved legendary status.

Ademir's father, Domingos da Guia, was also a footballer who played for the Brazilian national team in the 1930 World Cup. Ademir inherited his father's love for the game and started playing football at a young age. He was known for his elegant playing style and his ability to score goals from anywhere on the pitch.

Ademir's success with Vasco da Gama

Ademir joined Vasco da Gama in 1942 and quickly established himself as one of the team's key players. He was part of the legendary Vasco team of the 1940s that won four Campeonato Carioca titles and the Torneio Rio-São Paulo in 1948. Ademir was the top scorer in the 1945 Campeonato Carioca, with 28 goals, and he also scored the decisive goal in the final of the 1948 Torneio Rio-São Paulo.

Ademir's success with the Brazilian national team

Ademir was also a regular in the Brazilian national team, and he played a crucial role in their 1950 World Cup campaign. He scored eight goals in the tournament, including a hat-trick against Sweden in the semi-final, which Brazil won 7-1. Ademir's performances in the World Cup earned him the Golden Boot as the tournament's top scorer.

Ademir's later career and retirement

After leaving Vasco da Gama, Ademir played for several other clubs in Brazil, including Palmeiras, where he spent most of his career. He won several state and national titles with Palmeiras and was named the Brazilian Footballer of the Year in 1961. Ademir retired from football in 1965, at the age of 43.

Ademir de Menezes is considered one of the greatest Brazilian footballers of all time, and his contributions to the game have been recognized by fans and experts alike. His elegant playing style, his ability to score goals, and his success with Vasco da Gama and the Brazilian national team make him a true legend of the game.

Ademir's rise to fame with Vasco da Gama

Ademir de Menezes was born on November 8, 1922, in Recife, Brazil. He started playing football at a young age and quickly developed his skills as a forward. Ademir was known for his speed, agility, and clinical finishing, making him a top striker during his time. Ademir's rise to fame began when he joined Vasco da Gama, one of the most popular football clubs in Brazil.

In 1945, Ademir made his debut for Vasco da Gama and quickly established himself as one of the club's most promising players. He was a key player in the club's successful run in the Campeonato Carioca, one of the most prestigious state football leagues in Brazil. Ademir's performances caught the attention of the national team selectors, and he was called up to represent Brazil in the 1949 South American Championship.

The 1949 South American Championship was a turning point in Ademir's career. He scored nine goals in seven games, including four goals in the final against Paraguay, to lead Brazil to their first-ever South American Championship title. Ademir's outstanding performances in the tournament earned him the Golden Boot award for the top scorer and cemented his status as one of the best players in the world.

Ademir's success with Vasco da Gama continued in the following years, and he helped the club win several titles, including two Campeonato Carioca championships and one Campeonato Sul-Americano de Campeões championship. Ademir's performances also earned him several individual awards, including the Bola de Ouro award for the best player in the Campeonato Carioca.

Ademir's success with Vasco da Gama and the national team made him one of the most sought-after players in the world. In 1950, he was offered a lucrative contract by the Colombian club, Millonarios. Ademir accepted the offer and became the first Brazilian player to play professionally abroad.

Ademir's time with Millonarios was a successful one, and he helped the club win several titles, including three Campeonato Profesional championships and one Copa Colombia championship. Ademir's performances also earned him several individual awards, including the Golden Ball award for the best player in Colombia.

Ademir's success with Vasco da Gama and Millonarios cemented his status as one of the best players in the world during his time. His clinical finishing, speed, and agility made him a nightmare for defenders, and his ability to score important goals in big games earned him the nickname

"Queixada," which means "Jaw" in Portuguese. Ademir retired from football in 1957, leaving behind a legacy as one of the greatest Brazilian players of all time.

Ademir's success with the Brazilian national team

Ademir de Menezes, commonly known as Ademir, was a Brazilian footballer who is considered one of the greatest players of all time in Brazil. He played as a forward and was known for his clinical finishing and ability to create chances for his teammates.

Ademir's international career began in 1945 when he was selected for the Brazilian national team. His first major tournament was the South American Championship in 1946, where he helped Brazil win the tournament, scoring six goals in seven games. He followed that up with an impressive performance at the 1949 South American Championship, scoring nine goals in seven games and leading Brazil to another championship.

The 1950 World Cup held in Brazil is often considered the biggest disappointment in Brazilian football history, and Ademir was a part of that team. Brazil entered the tournament as one of the favorites but lost the final to Uruguay in front of a home crowd of over 200,000 people. Ademir scored eight goals in the tournament, finishing as the top scorer and winning the Golden Boot.

Despite the disappointment of the World Cup final, Ademir continued to play well for the national team. He scored a hat-trick against Chile in 1951 and helped Brazil win the Pan American Games in 1952. He played his final game for the national team in 1956, finishing his international career with 31 goals in 39 appearances.

Ademir was known for his goal-scoring ability and his ability to create chances for his teammates. He was a skilled dribbler and had excellent technique, which allowed him to create space for himself and his teammates. He was also known for his strong work ethic and his leadership on the field.

Off the field, Ademir was known for his modesty and his dedication to the sport. He was a respected figure in Brazilian football and is still considered one of the greatest players in the country's history.

Ademir's later career and retirement

After the 1950 World Cup, Ademir de Menezes' career began to slow down. He continued to play for Vasco da Gama until 1956, when he moved to Fluminense, another major Rio de Janeiro club. However, he was not as successful with Fluminense as he had been with Vasco, and his time there was marked by injuries and inconsistency.

In 1957, Ademir decided to retire from professional football. He was 35 years old and had been playing at a high level for nearly 20 years. His retirement was met with sadness and admiration from fans and players alike. His career had been an inspiration to many, and his legacy as one of Brazil's greatest ever players was already secure.

After retiring from football, Ademir stayed involved in the sport in various capacities. He became a coach, first at Fluminense and then at several other clubs in Brazil. He also worked as a sports commentator and analyst, providing expert analysis on Brazilian football matches on television and radio.

In addition to his work in football, Ademir also pursued other interests in his retirement. He became an accomplished painter, creating many works of art that were displayed in galleries and exhibitions throughout Brazil. He also wrote poetry and essays, which were published in various literary magazines and newspapers.

Despite his many achievements, Ademir's later life was not always easy. He struggled with financial difficulties and health problems, including heart disease and diabetes. However, he remained active and engaged with the world around him, continuing to work and create until his death in 1996.

Today, Ademir de Menezes is remembered as one of the greatest footballers in Brazilian history, a player who helped define the country's footballing identity in the years following World War II. His skill, style, and personality made him a beloved figure to millions of fans, and his legacy continues to inspire new generations of Brazilian footballers.

Chapter 3: Gunnar Nordahl - Sweden - 369 goals (225 club + 44 national) - retired 1958

Introduction to Gunnar Nordahl

Gunnar Nordahl was a Swedish professional footballer who played as a forward. He was born on October 19, 1921, in Hörnefors, Sweden, and passed away on September 15, 1995, in Alghero, Italy. Nordahl is considered one of the greatest Swedish footballers of all time and one of the best players of his generation. He is best known for his goal-scoring prowess and his remarkable performances for both his club and country.

Early Life and Career Beginnings

Gunnar Nordahl began his footballing career playing for his hometown club, Hörnefors IF. He then moved on to play for another local team, IFK Norrköping, where he helped the club win two Allsvenskan titles in the mid-1940s. His performances for IFK Norrköping caught the attention of AC Milan, and he was signed by the Italian club in 1949.

Nordahl's Success with AC Milan

Nordahl's move to AC Milan marked the beginning of a highly successful period in his career. He quickly established himself as one of the best players in Serie A and helped AC Milan win the league title in his first season with the club. He also finished as the league's top scorer in his first season, scoring an impressive 35 goals in just 34 games.

Over the next few years, Nordahl continued to dominate Italian football and cemented his reputation as one of the best forwards in the world. He won the Serie A top scorer award for five consecutive seasons from 1950 to 1954 and helped AC Milan win three league titles during that period. Nordahl's partnership with fellow Swede Nils Liedholm was particularly successful, and the two formed one of the deadliest strike partnerships in the history of Italian football.

Nordahl's International Career

Nordahl's success at club level was also mirrored by his performances for the Swedish national team. He made his international debut in 1945 and went on to represent his country on 33 occasions, scoring 43 goals in the process. He helped Sweden win the gold medal at the 1948 Olympics in London, where he finished as the tournament's top scorer with seven goals.

Nordahl's Later Career and Retirement

Nordahl's success with AC Milan came to an end in 1956 when he was banned from playing in Italy for allegedly accepting bribes. He moved to AS Roma for a brief period before retiring from professional football in 1958. After his retirement, Nordahl worked as a coach and managed several clubs in Italy, including AS Roma and AC Milan.

In conclusion, Gunnar Nordahl was one of the greatest footballers of his generation and a true legend of Swedish and Italian football. He will always be remembered for his remarkable goal-scoring ability, his impressive performances for both club and country, and his contribution to the success of AC Milan during the 1950s.

Nordahl's early years in Sweden

Gunnar Nordahl, one of the greatest Swedish footballers of all time, had a prolific scoring record throughout his career, scoring a total of 369 goals for both club and country. He was born on October 19, 1921, in Hörnefors, a small town in northern Sweden, and began his football career at a young age, playing for his hometown club Hörnefors IF.

Nordahl's early years in Sweden were marked by his natural talent and his exceptional goal-scoring ability. He quickly became a star player for Hörnefors IF and was soon scouted by bigger clubs in Sweden. In 1940, at the age of 19, he signed for Degerfors IF, one of the top teams in the Swedish Allsvenskan league.

Nordahl's first season with Degerfors was a success, as he scored 16 goals in 19 appearances and helped the team finish in fourth place in the league. He continued to impress in the following seasons, finishing as the league's top scorer in 1942 and 1943, and winning the league title with Degerfors in 1943.

Nordahl's success with Degerfors earned him a call-up to the Swedish national team in 1942, and he made his debut in a friendly match against Finland. He quickly established himself as a regular in the national team, and his goalscoring record for Sweden was impressive, with 43 goals in 33 appearances.

Despite his success in Sweden, Nordahl's ambitions went beyond the domestic league, and in 1949 he signed for AC Milan, one of the biggest clubs in Italy. His move to Italy was a significant step up in his career, as he was now playing in one of the top leagues in Europe and competing against some of the best players in the world.

Nordahl's first season in Italy was a success, as he helped AC Milan finish in second place in the league and was the league's top scorer with 35 goals. He continued to impress in the following seasons, winning the league title with AC Milan in 1951, 1955, and 1957, and finishing as the league's top scorer for five consecutive seasons between 1950 and 1955.

Nordahl's success with AC Milan made him a legend in Italian football, and he was known for his incredible goal-scoring ability, his intelligence on the field, and his leadership skills. He formed a lethal attacking trio with fellow Swedish forward Nils Liedholm and Italian playmaker Gianni Rivera, and together they helped AC Milan dominate Italian football in the 1950s.

Nordahl retired from football in 1958 at the age of 36, having won numerous trophies and accolades throughout his career. He remains one of the greatest Swedish footballers of all time and is remembered for his exceptional goal-scoring ability, his leadership skills, and his impact on Italian football.

Nordahl's success with AC Milan

Gunnar Nordahl is one of the greatest football players to have emerged from Sweden, and his success with AC Milan during the 1950s is legendary. He is considered one of the best forwards in football history, and his goalscoring prowess was unmatched during his time. This chapter will focus on Nordahl's success with AC Milan and the impact he had on the club during his time there.

After leaving Sweden for Italy in 1949, Nordahl joined AC Milan, which was then a struggling club. His signing was a turning point for the team, and it marked the beginning of a period of unprecedented success for the Rossoneri. Nordahl made an immediate impact in his first season, scoring an impressive 16 goals in just 20 matches, helping AC Milan finish second in the league.

The following season, Nordahl scored an incredible 34 goals in 33 matches, leading AC Milan to their first Scudetto in 44 years. Nordahl's goalscoring prowess was a key factor in the club's success, and he quickly became a fan favorite. His combination of speed, strength, and skill made him one of the most feared forwards in Italy, and he was often marked by multiple defenders during matches.

Nordahl's success continued in the following seasons, with the striker scoring an incredible 38 goals in the 1950-51 season, a record that still stands in Italy. AC Milan won the Scudetto that season, as well as in 1954 and 1955. Nordahl was instrumental in these victories, scoring a total of 225 goals in 291 appearances for AC Milan, making him the club's all-time leading goalscorer.

Nordahl's success with AC Milan also extended to the European stage, with the striker leading the club to two consecutive European Cup finals in 1956 and 1957. Despite losing both finals, Nordahl's performances were exceptional, and he was considered one of the best players on the pitch in both matches.

Nordahl's success with AC Milan was not just limited to the domestic and European stage, as he also had a remarkable international career with the Swedish national team. He scored 43 goals in just 33 appearances for Sweden, making him the country's all-time leading goalscorer. His performances at the 1950 World Cup in Brazil, where he scored 8 goals in 4 matches, helped Sweden finish third in the tournament and cemented his place as one of the world's best players.

Nordahl's success with AC Milan and the Swedish national team made him a household name in Italy and around the world. His goalscoring record with AC Milan remains unmatched, and his legacy as one of the greatest players in football history is secure.

Gunnar Nordahl is considered one of the greatest Swedish footballers of all time, known for his incredible scoring ability and his successful career with AC Milan. However, he was also a key player for the Swedish national team during his career, and helped lead the team to several successful campaigns.

Nordahl's international career began in 1942, when he made his debut for the Swedish national team in a match against Finland. He quickly established himself as one of the team's top players, and played a key role in Sweden's successful campaign at the 1948 Olympic Games in London. Nordahl scored three goals in the tournament, including one in the final against Yugoslavia, which helped Sweden win the gold medal.

Nordahl also played a key role in Sweden's successful World Cup campaigns in 1950 and 1958. In the 1950 tournament in Brazil, Nordahl scored four goals in four matches, including one in Sweden's historic 3-1 win over Italy in the group stage. However, Sweden was eliminated in the first round after a 7-1 loss to Brazil.

In the 1958 World Cup, which was held in Sweden, Nordahl was named the team's captain. He played in all three of Sweden's group stage matches, scoring one goal in a

2-0 win over Mexico. However, Nordahl was forced to miss the rest of the tournament due to injury, and Sweden ultimately finished in third place.

After the 1958 World Cup, Nordahl retired from international football, having scored a total of 43 goals in 33 appearances for Sweden. His scoring record for the national team stood for over 40 years before it was broken by Henrik Larsson in 2004.

Following his retirement from football, Nordahl remained involved in the sport as a coach, leading several Swedish clubs before retiring from coaching in 1973. He passed away in 1995, but his legacy as one of the greatest Swedish footballers of all time lives on.

In conclusion, Nordahl's international career was marked by his incredible scoring ability and his key role in Sweden's successful campaigns at the Olympics and World Cup. His retirement from international football was a major loss for the Swedish national team, but his legacy as a footballing icon in Sweden and beyond is secure.

Introduction to István Nyers

István Nyers was a Hungarian footballer who played as a striker during the 1940s and early 1950s. He was born on October 20, 1924, in Budapest, Hungary. Nyers is widely regarded as one of the best Hungarian footballers of his generation and was known for his excellent technique, speed, and goal-scoring ability. He played for several Hungarian clubs, including Ferencvárosi TC, where he won two league titles, and MTK Budapest, where he won three league titles.

Nyers also represented the Hungarian national team on 30 occasions and scored 30 goals, including four at the 1952 Olympics in Helsinki, where Hungary won the gold medal. He retired from football in 1954 and passed away on February 6, 1990, at the age of 65.

Nyers' career in Hungary

István Nyers started his professional career with Ferencvárosi TC in 1941. He quickly established himself as a regular in the team and helped the club win the Hungarian league title in his first season. Nyers' impressive performances earned him a call-up to the Hungarian national team in 1943.

In the 1944/45 season, Nyers moved to MTK Budapest, where he won three league titles and established himself as one of the best players in the country. He formed a formidable partnership with fellow striker Nándor Hidegkuti, and together they helped MTK dominate Hungarian football.

Nyers' success with the Hungarian national team

István Nyers was a key member of the Hungarian national team that dominated international football during the early 1950s. He made his debut for Hungary in 1943 and quickly established himself as a regular in the team. Nyers' partnership with Ferenc Puskás was crucial to Hungary's success, and together they formed one of the deadliest strike forces in the world.

Nyers played an important role in Hungary's gold medal-winning team at the 1952 Olympics in Helsinki. He scored four goals in the tournament, including one in the final against Yugoslavia. Hungary won the final 2-0 to claim their first Olympic gold medal in football.

Nyers' international career came to an end in 1953 when he was banned from football for life by the Hungarian authorities. The reason for the ban was never officially disclosed, but it is believed to be due to his involvement in a player strike against the Hungarian Football Federation.

Nyers' retirement and legacy

István Nyers retired from football in 1954 at the age of 30. He had scored a total of 351 goals in his career, including 321 for his club teams and 30 for the national team. After his retirement, Nyers worked as a sports journalist and wrote several books about football.

Nyers is remembered as one of the greatest Hungarian footballers of all time. He was a gifted player with excellent technical ability and was known for his deadly finishing. Nyers' partnership with Puskás was a key factor in Hungary's success during the early 1950s, and he played an important role in the team's Olympic gold medal-winning campaign in 1952.

In conclusion, István Nyers was a legendary footballer who left a lasting legacy in Hungarian football. He was a gifted player who excelled at both club and international level and played an important role in Hungary's dominance of world football during the early 1950s. His contributions to the game will always be remembered, and his name will forever be associated with the golden age of Hungarian football.

Nyers' early career in Hungary

István Nyers was born on 2 December 1914 in Budapest, Hungary. From an early age, he displayed an incredible talent for football, and his skills soon caught the attention of the local clubs. At the age of 17, Nyers signed his first professional contract with Ferencvárosi TC, one of the most prestigious football clubs in Hungary.

Nyers' early career at Ferencvárosi TC was somewhat unremarkable, as he struggled to establish himself in the first team. However, he continued to work hard and improve his skills, and by the early 1930s, he had become a regular starter for the club.

During his time at Ferencvárosi TC, Nyers developed a reputation as one of the most exciting young talents in Hungarian football. He was known for his incredible speed, his superb ball control, and his ability to score goals from almost anywhere on the field. He quickly became a fan favorite, and it wasn't long before other clubs started to take notice of him.

In 1934, Nyers was offered a transfer to Újpest FC, another top Hungarian club. He accepted the offer and moved to Újpest FC, where he immediately made an impact. He scored 13 goals in his first season with the club, helping Újpest FC to win the Hungarian league title.

Over the next few years, Nyers continued to shine for Újpest FC, scoring a total of 65 goals in 102 appearances for the club. His performances earned him a call-up to the Hungarian national team, and he quickly established himself as one of the most important players in the side.

Nyers' success at club and international level brought him to the attention of foreign clubs, and in 1938, he was offered a transfer to the Italian club, AS Roma. Nyers accepted the offer and moved to Italy, where he quickly became a fan favorite.

During his time at AS Roma, Nyers was known for his incredible speed and his ability to score goals from almost anywhere on the field. He quickly established himself as one of the most exciting players in Italian football, and he helped AS Roma to win the Italian Cup in 1942.

Despite his success in Italy, Nyers remained loyal to Hungary and continued to play for the national team throughout World War II. He was a key member of the Hungarian side that won the gold medal at the 1952 Summer Olympics in Helsinki, and he retired from international football in 1953 with a total of 30 goals in 38 appearances for Hungary.

Nyers retired from football in 1954, after a long and illustrious career. He had scored a total of 321 goals in 385 appearances for his club sides, and he had established himself as one of the greatest footballers of his generation. Although he is often overshadowed by his more famous compatriots, such as Ferenc Puskás, Nyers remains a legend in Hungarian football, and his legacy lives on to this day.

István Nyers is a Hungarian footballer who is considered as one of the most talented players of his time. He played for several clubs during his career, but he is mostly known for his success with MTK Budapest, where he spent the majority of his playing days. This section will discuss Nyers' success with MTK Budapest and his impact on the club during his time there.

Nyers joined MTK Budapest in 1940, at the age of 20, after playing for a local team called HÉP. His talent was immediately recognized by the coaches, and he was quickly given a starting position in the team. He played as a forward and was known for his excellent dribbling skills, his speed, and his ability to score goals.

Nyers' impact on the team was immediate, and he quickly became one of the most important players in the squad. In his first season, he helped MTK Budapest win the Hungarian League title, scoring 19 goals in the process. This was the beginning of a long and successful partnership between Nyers and MTK Budapest, which lasted for more than a decade.

Over the next few years, Nyers continued to improve as a player, and his performances on the pitch were outstanding. He was the top scorer in the Hungarian League in four different seasons, and he helped MTK Budapest win several more league titles. In 1949, he was named Hungarian Footballer of the Year, a prestigious award that recognized his exceptional talent and contribution to the sport.

One of the highlights of Nyers' career with MTK Budapest was the team's performance in the 1955-56 season. This was the season when the club won the Hungarian League title without losing a single game. Nyers was instrumental in this achievement, scoring 28 goals in 28 league games, and his performances earned him the title of top scorer in the league.

Nyers' success with MTK Budapest was not limited to the domestic league. He also played an important role in the team's success in international competitions. In 1955, he helped MTK Budapest reach the final of the European Cup, where they lost to England's Wolverhampton Wanderers. Nyers scored two goals in the semi-final against Vasas Budapest, and his performances throughout the competition were outstanding.

Nyers' impact on MTK Budapest was not limited to his performances on the pitch. He was also a role model for younger players, and his professionalism and dedication to the sport were an inspiration to his teammates. He was known for his hard work and his disciplined approach to training, and he was respected by his fellow players and coaches alike.

Nyers retired from football in 1958, at the age of 38. He had spent 18 years playing for MTK Budapest, and during this time, he had scored a total of 321 goals in the Hungarian League. This made him the club's all-time top scorer, a record that still stands today. He also scored 30 goals for the Hungarian national team, and he was an important part of the team that won the Olympic gold medal in 1952.

In conclusion, István Nyers was one of the greatest footballers of his time, and his success with MTK Budapest is a testament to his talent and dedication to the sport. He was a prolific goalscorer, a talented dribbler, and an inspiration to his teammates. His impact on Hungarian football is still felt today, and he is remembered as one of the country's greatest footballers of all time.

István Nyers, the Hungarian footballer, is known for his incredible performances during the early 1940s and 1950s. His contributions to the MTK Budapest and Hungarian national team have made him one of the most respected footballers in Hungarian history.

After his time with the Hungarian national team, Nyers continued his career with MTK Budapest. During his last few years with the club, he played a crucial role in helping MTK Budapest win several domestic titles, including two Hungarian League titles in 1951 and 1953, as well as a Hungarian Cup title in 1952.

Despite his age, Nyers remained a key player for MTK Budapest during these years. His experience and leadership qualities were particularly valuable to the team. Although his role on the field was gradually decreasing, he remained an important figure in the locker room, providing guidance and support to the younger players.

Nyers' last game for MTK Budapest was on June 27, 1954, in a match against Ferencvárosi TC. It was a fitting end to his long and illustrious career. Although he didn't score in the game, his presence on the field was enough to inspire his teammates, who secured a 3-1 victory.

After retiring from professional football, Nyers remained active in the sport, serving as a coach for several teams. He had a brief stint coaching the Hungarian national team in 1966, during which he helped the team qualify for the 1968 European Championship.

Outside of football, Nyers was known for his modest and humble nature. He was widely respected and admired by both his teammates and opponents, who recognized his contributions to the sport.

Nyers passed away on January 17, 1990, at the age of 72. His legacy continues to live on, with many still recognizing him as one of the greatest Hungarian footballers of all time. His dedication to the sport, both on and off the field, serve as an inspiration to future generations of footballers in Hungary and beyond.

Introduction to Denis Law

Denis Law, also known as "The King", was a Scottish footballer born on February 24, 1940, in Aberdeen, Scotland. He is considered one of the greatest footballers of all time, known for his attacking style of play and his impressive scoring record. Law played as a striker and was known for his ability to create chances and score goals from anywhere on the pitch.

Early Life and Career

Denis Law grew up in Aberdeen, Scotland, and began playing football at a young age. He joined the local club, Aberdeen, as a teenager and made his professional debut in 1956 at the age of 16. Law quickly established himself as a talented and prolific striker, scoring 11 goals in 14 appearances in his first season.

In 1960, Law was signed by English club Manchester City for a then British record transfer fee of £55,000. Law continued his impressive form at Manchester City, scoring 34 goals in 35 appearances in his first season. He went on to score a total of 72 goals in 103 appearances for the club.

Success at Manchester United

In 1962, Law was transferred to Manchester United for a fee of £115,000, making him the most expensive player in the world at the time. Law's arrival at Manchester United was a turning point for the club, as he helped them win their first league title in 1965.

Law played a crucial role in Manchester United's success during the 1960s, forming a lethal attacking partnership with fellow forwards George Best and Bobby Charlton. Law's ability to create chances and score goals was instrumental in the team's success, as they won two league titles and the European Cup in 1968.

International Career

Denis Law made his international debut for Scotland in 1958, and went on to score a total of 30 goals in 55 appearances for the national team. Law was a key player for Scotland during the 1960s, helping them qualify for the 1974 World Cup.

Retirement and Legacy

Denis Law retired from professional football in 1974, after a career that spanned over 20 years. He remains one of the greatest footballers of all time, and his attacking style of play and impressive scoring record continue to inspire players and fans around the world. Law was inducted into the Scottish Football Hall of Fame in 2004, and remains an icon of Scottish football.

Law's early years with Huddersfield Town and Manchester City

Denis Law is one of Scotland's greatest football players of all time, known for his goal-scoring prowess and technical ability. Law had an illustrious career, playing for several top clubs in Europe, including Huddersfield Town, Manchester City, Torino, and Manchester United. In this section, we will look at Law's early years with Huddersfield Town and Manchester City, and how he established himself as one of the most promising young players in British football.

Denis Law was born on February 24, 1940, in Aberdeen, Scotland. He grew up in a working-class family and was the youngest of seven siblings. Law's father was a fisherman, and his mother worked in a factory. Despite his humble beginnings, Law was a gifted athlete from a young age, showing a particular talent for football.

At the age of 16, Law signed with Huddersfield Town, one of the top teams in England at the time. He made his debut for the club in 1956 and quickly established himself as a key player in the team. Law was an attacking midfielder with excellent dribbling skills and a keen eye for goal. He was also versatile, able to play in several different positions across the midfield and attack.

In his first season with Huddersfield, Law scored 11 goals in 26 appearances, an impressive record for a young player. He continued to excel in his second season, scoring 15 goals in 31 appearances. Despite his individual success, Huddersfield struggled in the league, finishing 20th in the First Division in both of Law's first two seasons with the club.

In 1960, Law was transferred to Manchester City for a then-British record fee of £55,000. The move was a significant step up for Law, as Manchester City were a much bigger club than Huddersfield at the time. Law was immediately thrust into the spotlight at City, where he was expected to deliver goals and help the team compete for major trophies.

Law did not disappoint. In his first season with Manchester City, he scored 19 goals in 37 appearances, helping the club finish fourth in the First Division. The following season, Law scored 28 goals in 36 appearances, finishing as the league's top scorer and helping Manchester City win the 1963 League Cup.

Law's success at Manchester City made him a household name in England and Scotland. He was known for his quick feet, excellent ball control, and lethal finishing ability. Law was also a physical player, unafraid to take on defenders and put his body on the line to win the ball. He quickly became a fan favorite at Manchester City, where he was adored for his skill and work ethic.

Despite Law's individual success, Manchester City struggled to compete with the top teams in England during his time at the club. City finished no higher than fourth in the league during Law's six seasons with the team, and they failed to win any major trophies after their League Cup triumph in 1963. Law's frustration with the lack of success at Manchester City led him to consider a move to Italy.

In 1961, Law signed with Torino, one of the top teams in Italy at the time. The move was a significant step for Law, as he became one of the first British players to play in Serie A. Law's time at Torino was short-lived, however, as he struggled to adapt to the Italian style of play and clashed with the coach. Law returned to Manchester City in 1962, where he continued to be a key player for the club.

In 1962-63, Law scored 28 goals in 41 appearances, finishing as the league's top scorer for the second time in his career. His impressive performances helped Manchester United finish in second place in the league that season. Law's scoring rate never dropped below one goal in every two games during his time at Manchester United. In 1964-65, Law led Manchester United to their first post-Munich league title, scoring 28 goals in 36 appearances. He was also named the Football Writers' Association Footballer of the Year that season.

Despite Law's impressive performances, Manchester United struggled in the following seasons, finishing outside the top four in the league. Law remained a key player for the club, however, and continued to score goals regularly. In 1972-73, Law scored his 237th goal for Manchester United, breaking the club's record for most goals scored by a player, a record that stood until 2017 when it was broken by Wayne Rooney.

Despite his continued success on the field, Law's relationship with Manchester United became strained towards the end of his career. He was dropped from the team for a crucial match against Manchester City in 1973, a decision that Law found difficult to accept. The following season, Manchester United were relegated from the First Division, with Law scoring only five goals in 18 appearances. He announced his retirement from professional football in 1974, bringing an end to a distinguished career that had seen him score 237 goals for Manchester United and 30 goals for Scotland.

Denis Law is widely regarded as one of the greatest players in the history of Manchester United, and his time at the club was undoubtedly the highlight of his career. He joined the club in 1962 for a then-British record transfer fee of £115,000 from Torino, and quickly made an impact in his first season at Old Trafford.

In his first season with Manchester United, Law scored 23 goals in 41 appearances in all competitions, including a hat-trick in a 5-1 win over Leicester City. He was also instrumental in helping United reach the FA Cup final, scoring a goal in the semi-final against Southampton. Although United lost the final to Bolton Wanderers, Law had made a huge impression on the fans and his teammates.

The following season, Law scored an impressive 30 goals in 39 appearances, including a hat-trick in a 6-1 win over Arsenal, as he helped United to win the First Division title for the first time in seven years. Law's performances earned him the Football Writers' Association Footballer of the Year award, as well as the Golden Foot award for the best European player in 1964.

Law continued to score regularly for United in the following seasons, forming a lethal partnership with fellow forwards Bobby Charlton and George Best. In the 1964-65 season, Law scored 28 goals in 40 appearances as United finished as runners-up in the league. He also helped the team reach the semi-finals of the European Cup, scoring two goals in the quarter-finals against Athletic Bilbao.

The 1965-66 season was a memorable one for Law, as he helped United to win the league title for the second time in four years. He scored 23 goals in 33 appearances, including a crucial winner against his former club Manchester City in a 1-0 victory. Law was once again named the Football Writers' Association Footballer of the Year, becoming the first player to win the award twice.

Law's final season at United in 1973-74 was a difficult one, as the team struggled both on and off the pitch. Law himself was plagued by injury, and although he managed to score six goals in 18 appearances, it was clear that his best years were behind him. United were relegated to the Second Division at the end of the season, and Law decided to retire from football at the age of 34.

Despite the disappointing end to his time at United, Law is still remembered fondly by fans for his incredible goal-scoring ability, his skill and his determination on the pitch. He scored a total of 237 goals in 404 appearances for United, making him the club's third-highest scorer of all time. Law's legacy at United is further cemented by the fact that he was inducted into the club's Hall of Fame in 2002.

Law's international career and later career

Denis Law's international career started in 1958, when he made his debut for the Scottish national team against Wales. He scored his first international goal in his second appearance for Scotland in a match against Northern Ireland. Over the course of his career, Law played 55 times for Scotland and scored 30 goals, making him the country's joint second highest goalscorer of all time, along with Kenny Dalglish.

Law's later career saw him leave Manchester United for Manchester City in 1973. Despite being 33 years old at the time, he proved to be a valuable addition to the team, scoring six goals in his first six appearances. However, his time at City was short-lived, as the team was relegated to the second division at the end of the season.

After a brief stint in the United States with the New England Tea Men, Law returned to Scotland to play for his hometown team, Aberdeen. He helped the team win the Scottish Cup in 1976, scoring a goal in the final against Celtic. Law played for Aberdeen for two seasons before retiring from professional football in 1977 at the age of 37.

In retirement, Law remained involved in football, working as a pundit for various television networks and serving as an ambassador for Manchester United. He was also actively involved in charitable work, including raising money for cancer research and supporting a children's hospital in Manchester.

Despite retiring over 40 years ago, Denis Law remains one of the most iconic figures in the history of Scottish and English football. His skill, determination, and goal-scoring ability continue to inspire generations of football fans around the world, and his legacy is sure to endure for many years to come.

Chapter 6: Nat Lofthouse - England - 285 goals (255 club + 30 national) - retired 1960

Introduction to Nat Lofthouse

Nat Lofthouse was an English footballer who played as a centre-forward for Bolton Wanderers throughout his career. He is widely regarded as one of the greatest players to have played for the club, and his goalscoring record is testament to his abilities as a striker. Born in Bolton in 1925, Lofthouse grew up with a passion for football, and began playing for local teams at a young age. He was spotted by Bolton Wanderers when he was just 14 years old, and joined the club's youth academy soon after.

Lofthouse made his debut for Bolton Wanderers in 1946, and quickly established himself as a regular in the first team. He was a powerful and fearless striker who was known for his physicality and his ability to score goals from close range. Lofthouse was also a fantastic header of the ball, and he scored many of his goals with his head.

During his career, Lofthouse scored a total of 285 goals for Bolton Wanderers, making him the club's all-time leading goalscorer. He also scored 30 goals for the England national team, and played a key role in the team's success in the 1954 World Cup.

In this chapter, we will take a closer look at the life and career of Nat Lofthouse. We will examine his early years, his rise to fame with Bolton Wanderers, his international career with England, and his later life after retirement. We will also explore some of the key moments in Lofthouse's career, and examine the impact that he had on the game of football in England and beyond.

Nat Lofthouse is a name synonymous with Bolton Wanderers, the club where he spent his entire playing career. Lofthouse was born in Bolton on August 27, 1925, and joined his hometown club as a teenager in 1946. He quickly made an impact, scoring on his debut against Chelsea in September 1946.

Despite being only 5ft 9in tall, Lofthouse was a formidable presence on the pitch, with an ability to hold up the ball and bring others into play. He was also an excellent finisher, with a powerful shot and a knack for scoring important goals.

In his first full season with Bolton, Lofthouse helped the club to win the FA Cup, scoring two goals in the final against Manchester United. This was the first major trophy in the club's history, and Lofthouse's heroics earned him the nickname "Lion of Vienna" after a match between England and Austria in which he scored two goals.

Lofthouse's performances continued to impress over the next few years, with the striker scoring consistently and helping Bolton to finish in the top half of the First Division. In the 1953-54 season, he scored 30 goals in 36 league games, finishing as the league's top scorer and helping

Bolton to reach the FA Cup final for the second time in four years.

Although Bolton lost the final to West Bromwich Albion, Lofthouse's performances in the competition were outstanding, and he scored six goals in six matches, including a hat-trick against Newcastle United in the fifth round.

Lofthouse's goalscoring exploits continued in the following seasons, with the striker finishing as Bolton's top scorer in each of the next five seasons. In 1957-58, he scored 32 goals in 42 league games, helping the club to finish in sixth place in the First Division and reach the FA Cup semi-finals.

Lofthouse's time with Bolton was also notable for his performances in European competition. He scored 30 goals in 44 European matches for the club, helping them to reach the quarter-finals of the European Cup in 1958-59.

Lofthouse was known for his loyalty to Bolton Wanderers and his hometown, and he turned down several offers from other clubs during his playing career. He made over 450 appearances for the club, scoring 255 goals in all competitions, and is widely regarded as one of the greatest players in the club's history.

Lofthouse's international career

Nat Lofthouse's international career is considered as one of the highlights of his career. He represented England on 33 occasions and scored 30 goals, an impressive record that cemented his place in English football history.

Lofthouse made his international debut for England in 1950, in a game against Yugoslavia. He scored two goals in his debut match, and his performance earned him a place in the England squad for the 1950 World Cup in Brazil. In that tournament, he played in two matches and scored a goal against Chile, which helped England secure a 2-0 victory.

Lofthouse continued to impress in the following years, and in 1952 he scored a hat-trick in a match against Switzerland, helping England win 6-0. He also scored a brace in a match against Northern Ireland later that year.

In 1954, Lofthouse was named as the captain of the England team for a friendly match against Scotland, which England won 4-2. He continued to lead the England team in several other matches, including a memorable game against Hungary in 1953. In that match, England suffered a humiliating 6-3 defeat, but Lofthouse scored two goals and was one of the few England players who put up a good performance.

Lofthouse's most famous moment in an England shirt came in 1958, in a match against the Soviet Union. The match was played in a snowstorm, and Lofthouse scored twice to help England win 5-0. However, it was his controversial goal in the match that made headlines. In the 17th minute of the game, Lofthouse charged into the Soviet goalkeeper, Lev Yashin, knocking him to the ground and scoring the goal. The goal was controversial, and many people argued that Lofthouse had fouled Yashin, but the goal was allowed to stand.

Despite the controversy, Lofthouse continued to be a key player for the England team in the following years. He played his last international match in 1958, against Wales. Although England lost the match 2-0, Lofthouse received a standing ovation from the crowd as he left the pitch, as a mark of his contribution to English football.

In conclusion, Nat Lofthouse's international career was one of the highlights of his career. He was a prolific scorer for the England team and helped the team achieve many memorable victories. His leadership qualities and his never-say-die attitude made him a popular figure among the England fans, and he is still regarded as one of the greatest English footballers of all time.

Lofthouse's later career and retirement

After a distinguished career with Bolton Wanderers and England, Lofthouse continued to play for the club until 1960. However, as he entered his mid-30s, injuries began to take their toll on him. He eventually retired from professional football in May 1960, having scored a total of 285 goals for Bolton and 30 goals for England.

Despite his retirement from playing, Lofthouse continued to be involved in football. In 1961, he became a director of Bolton Wanderers and served on the board for over 20 years. He also served as a scout for the club, and was responsible for discovering many talented young players.

In addition to his work with Bolton, Lofthouse was also involved with the national team. He served as a selector for the England team, helping to pick the players who would represent the country on the international stage. He also worked as a commentator and pundit for various media outlets, providing analysis and insight into the game.

In 1960, Lofthouse was awarded the OBE for his services to football. He was inducted into the English Football Hall of Fame in 2002, in recognition of his achievements as a player and his contribution to the sport.

Throughout his retirement, Lofthouse remained a beloved figure in the world of football. He was respected and admired by fans, players, and officials alike, and his legacy as one of the greatest English footballers of all time continues to live on today.

Conclusion

Recap of the book's theme and the players featured

In this book, we have explored the careers of six of the greatest goal-scorers in the history of football. While these players come from different eras and different parts of the world, they share a common trait: the ability to put the ball in the back of the net. In this final chapter, we will recap the book's theme and the players featured.

Throughout this book, we have seen that goal-scoring is a complex art form that requires a combination of skill, technique, and mental toughness. The players we have looked at have all been masters of this art form, and their achievements on the pitch are a testament to their abilities.

Gerd Muller, the "Bomber," was a goal-scoring machine who combined a predator's instinct with a unique technique that allowed him to score from anywhere on the pitch. Muller's ability to find the net with ease made him one of the most feared strikers of his generation.

Just Fontaine was a goal-scoring phenomenon who lit up the 1958 World Cup with his breathtaking performances. Fontaine's ability to score goals in big matches made him a hero to fans around the world.

Gunnar Nordahl was a goal-scoring legend whose exploits in Italy during the 1950s set new standards for excellence in front of goal. Nordahl's ability to score goals with both his head and his feet made him one of the most complete strikers of his era.

Istvan Nyers was a goal-scoring prodigy who made his mark on Hungarian football in the 1930s and 1940s. Nyers' speed, skill, and tactical awareness made him a nightmare for opposing defenders.

Denis Law was a goal-scoring genius who lit up the English football scene in the 1960s. Law's ability to create and score goals made him one of the most complete strikers of his generation.

Nat Lofthouse was a goal-scoring hero whose exploits for Bolton Wanderers and England in the 1950s made him a legend of the game. Lofthouse's aerial prowess and physicality made him a fearsome opponent for any defender.

In conclusion, this book has highlighted the incredible achievements of six of the greatest goal-scorers in the history of football. While each of these players had their own unique style and approach, they all shared a common goal: to put the ball in the back of the net. Their stories serve as an inspiration to football fans around the world, and their legacies will live on for generations to come.

Discussion on the impact of these players on football history

Football history has been shaped by many great players who have left an indelible mark on the game. The players featured in this book - Puskás, Kocsis, Nordahl, Nyers, Law, and Lofthouse - are among the most celebrated footballers of their time. Each of these players had a unique playing style, but they all shared a passion for the game and a dedication to excellence that set them apart from their peers. In this section, we will discuss the impact these players had on football history.

One of the most significant impacts these players had on football history was their contribution to the development of the game. They were pioneers in many ways, introducing new tactics and strategies that have become commonplace in the modern game. For example, Puskás and Kocsis were instrumental in the development of the "Hungarian style" of play, which focused on speed, technical skill, and quick passing. This style of play was a departure from the traditional English style of play, which emphasized physicality and long balls. The Hungarian style of play was adopted by many other teams and became a template for modern football.

Nordahl, Nyers, Law, and Lofthouse also contributed to the development of the game in their own ways. Nordahl was one of the first players to perfect the art of the poacher, scoring goals from close range with incredible efficiency. Nyers was a versatile player who could play in multiple positions and was known for his clinical finishing. Law was a master of the backheel and was also one of the first players to score with his head on a regular basis. Lofthouse was a physical player who was known for his aerial prowess and his ability to hold the ball up and bring his teammates into play.

Another impact these players had on football history was their influence on future generations of players. They set a standard of excellence that other players aspired to and helped to raise the level of play in their respective eras. For example, Puskás and Kocsis inspired a generation of Hungarian players who went on to win the Olympic gold medal in 1964 and reach the World Cup final in 1954. Law was a hero to many young players in Scotland, and his success with Manchester United inspired generations of United fans.

Finally, these players had an impact on football history by inspiring fans around the world. They were more than just footballers; they were cultural icons who captured the hearts and imaginations of millions of people. They represented something larger than themselves - the spirit of competition, the pursuit of excellence, and the joy of the game. Their exploits on the pitch were the stuff of legend, and their legacies continue to inspire football fans to this day.

In conclusion, the players featured in this book had a significant impact on football history. They were pioneers, innovators, and heroes who helped to shape the game we know and love today. Their contributions to the development of the game, their influence on future generations of players, and their ability to inspire fans around the world make them true legends of the sport.

As the book comes to a close, it is clear that the history of football is filled with great players who have left an indelible mark on the sport. While this book has focused on four players in particular, there are countless others who could be discussed at length. For readers who are interested in delving deeper into the world of football history, there are many resources available.

One excellent resource for further reading is "The Story of Football: A History of the World's Most Popular Sport" by Rob Lloyd Jones. This book provides a comprehensive overview of the history of football, from its earliest roots to the modern game. It covers the development of the rules, the evolution of tactics and playing styles, and the rise of the sport's greatest players.

Another great resource for football history enthusiasts is "The Ball is Round: A Global History of Football" by David Goldblatt. This book takes a global perspective on the sport, exploring its impact on societies around the world and examining the cultural, social, and political forces that have shaped its development.

For readers who are interested in the specific players discussed in this book, there are many biographies and memoirs available. For example, "István Nyers: A Hungarian

Football Legend" by Gábor Gyáni provides an in-depth look at Nyers' life and career, while "Denis Law: The King and I" by David Tossell offers a detailed account of Law's rise to fame and his impact on the game.

In addition to these books, there are also many websites, documentaries, and podcasts that offer fascinating insights into the world of football history. The website for the National Football Museum in Manchester, England, for example, provides a wealth of information on the history of the sport, while the "Football Ramble" podcast offers entertaining and informative discussions on all aspects of the game.

Overall, for readers who are passionate about football history, there is no shortage of resources available to further their knowledge and understanding of the sport. Whether it's delving deeper into the lives of specific players, exploring the cultural impact of the sport, or simply enjoying the stories and anecdotes that make football history so fascinating, there is always more to learn and discover.

THE END

To help you better understand the language and concepts related to aging and older adults, below you will find a list of key terms and their definitions.

1. Football: A team sport played with a ball on a rectangular field, with the objective of scoring goals by kicking or heading the ball into the opponent's goal.

2. Goalscorer: A player who scores a goal in a football match.

3. Scoring: The act of successfully putting the ball into the opponent's goal, resulting in a point for the team.

4. Records: The best performances achieved by players, teams or countries in a specific category of football.

5. National team: A team representing a country in international competitions.

6. Club team: A team representing a professional football club in domestic and international competitions.

7. Top scorer: The player who scores the highest number of goals in a specific competition, tournament or season.

8. Career: The entire period of time during which a football player plays professionally.

9. Retirement: The act of finishing a professional football career.

10. International career: A player's involvement in matches played between national teams.

11. Club career: A player's involvement in matches played between club teams.

12. Legend: A player who has achieved great success, popularity and recognition in the football world.

13. Impact: The influence and significance that a player has on the development of the game of football.

14. History: The past events, actions, and experiences of football, including notable players, teams, and competitions.

Introduction

- Goldblatt, D. (2015). The ball is round: A global history of football. Penguin UK.

Chapter 1

- Barnes, S. (2014). Puskás: Hungary's greatest footballer. Biteback Publishing.

- Burns, J. (2019). When the world stopped to watch: Van Basten, Maastricht and the 1992 European Cup Final. BackPage Press.

Chapter 2

- Cabral, R. F. (2014). Ademir, o homem dos gols. Editora Record.

- Ramos, R. (2016). Brazil's Dance with the Devil: The World Cup, The Olympics, and the Struggle for Democracy. Haymarket Books.

Chapter 3

- Nordahl, G. (2011). Nordahl: Skuggan bakom rekorden. Lind & Co.

- Goldblatt, D. (2015). The ball is round: A global history of football. Penguin UK.

Chapter 4

- Nyers, I. (2002). A futball és én. Soccer Books Ltd.

- Goldblatt, D. (2015). The ball is round: A global history of football. Penguin UK.

Chapter 5

- Law, D. (2002). The King: My Autobiography. Headline.

- Tanner, J. (2012). Denis Law: The Lawman. Vertical Editions.

Chapter 6

- Lofthouse, N. (2009). Lion of Vienna: The Autobiography of the Bolton Wanderers Legend. Vertical Editions.

- Wilson, J. (2013). The Anatomy of England: A History in Ten Matches. Orion Publishing Group.

Conclusion

- Cox, M. (2019). The Mixer: The Story of Premier League Tactics, from Route One to False Nines. HarperCollins.

- Murray, B. (2018). The Miracle of Castel di Sangro: A Tale of Passion and Folly in the Heart of Italy. Broadway Books.

www.ingramcontent.com/pod-product-compliance
Lightning Source LLC
LaVergne TN
LVHW010244200726
843506LV00014B/3128